Galapagos Landscapes

Scenic Photographs
from
Ecuador's Galapagos Archipelago,
the Encantadas or Enchanted Isles,
with words of
Herman Melville, Charles Darwin, and
HMS Beagle Captain Robert FitzRoy

by
Lynn Michelsohn
Photographs by Moses Michelsohn

Cleanan Press, Inc.
Roswell, New Mexico
USA

Galapagos Landscapes
Scenic Photographs from Ecuador's Galapagos Archipelago, the Encantadas or Enchanted Isles, with words of Herman Melville, Charles Darwin, and HMS Beagle Captain Robert FitzRoy

First Print Edition 1.2 C (9/15)
Also available as an ebook

Note: Some longer sections of early authors' writings have been broken into multiple paragraphs to improve readability. Their original spelling, grammar, and punctuation have been retained.

Published by: Cleanan Press, Inc., 401 West Vista Parkway, Roswell, NM 88201

Visit our website for more information about the Galapagos Islands and our other publications:

www.cleananpressBooks.com

Preface

Visitors have been arriving in the Galapagos Islands since at least 1535. While naturalist Charles Darwin made these volcanic peaks famous, Spanish explorers, English buccaneers (a fancy name for pirates), American whalers, Ecuadorian colonists, and a United States President have all put in appearances here over the centuries.

Herman Melville, author of *Moby-Dick*, was one such visitor. Like many before him, including Charles Darwin and Robert FitzRoy, he returned home to write about the strange worlds he found in the Enchanted Isles.

We hope these glimpses of its captivating natural history, through modern photographs combined with words written over 150 years ago by three famous fellow visitors, enrich your own stay in the Galapagos Archipelago.

Lynn Michelsohn
Moses Michelsohn

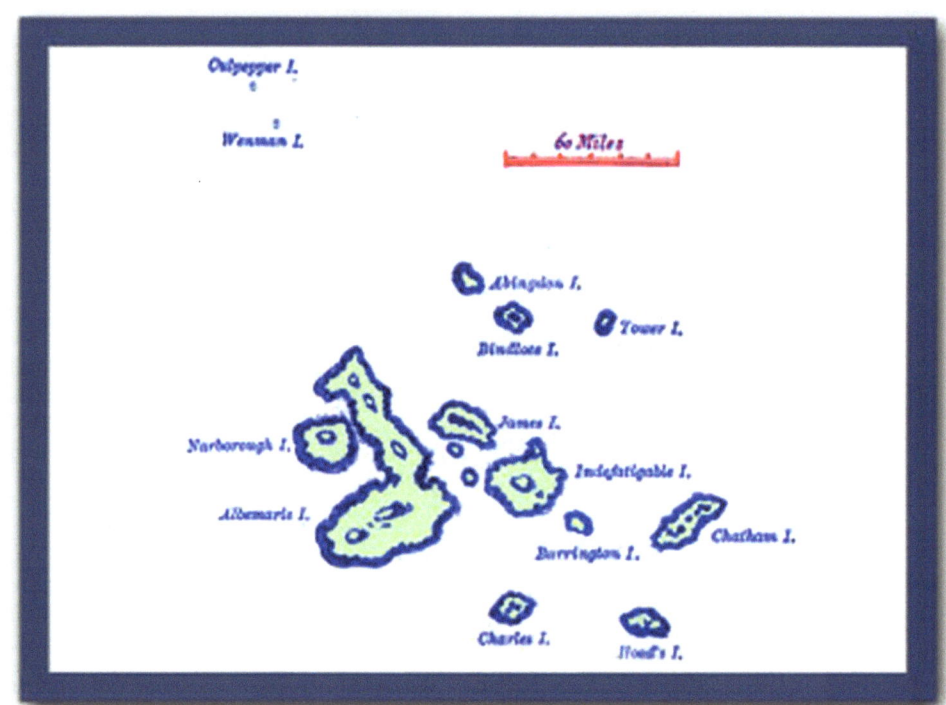

The Galapagos Islands

Table of Contents

HMS *Beagle* Captain Robert FitzRoy
and the Galapagos Islands

In December 1831, HMS Beagle, *captained by career Royal Navy officer Robert FitzRoy, set out from Plymouth, England, on an around-the-world survey voyage. Over the next five years, Captain FitzRoy, aided by his ship's crew including young British naturalist Charles Darwin, carried out his primary mission of charting landforms and currents of interest to navigation, especially those of South America.*

In 1839, Captain FitzRoy published his massive four volume Narrative of the Surveying Voyages of His Majesty's Ships *Adventure* and *Beagle*, between the Years 1826 and 1836, describing their Examination of the Southern Shores of South America, and the Beagle's Circumnavigation of the Globe. *In it, his brief introduction to the Galapagos Islands focused primarily on its climate, winds, and surrounding currents.*

A selection from Captain FitzRoy's Narrative . . .

The following day [7 September 1835] the *Beagle* left Callao, and steered direct towards the Galápagos Islands, of which, as they are novel ground, I shall be rather minute in my description.

. . .

There are six principal ones, nine smaller, and many islets scarcely deserving to be distinguished from mere rocks. The largest island is sixty miles in length, and about fifteen broad; the highest part being four thousand feet above the sea. All are of volcanic origin, and the lava, of which they are chiefly composed, is excessively hard.

Old Dampier (*Dampier's Voyage round the World*, 1681-1691, at the Galápagos in 1684) says, "The Spaniards, when they first discovered these islands, found multitudes of 'guanos' and land-turtle, or tortoise, and named them the Galápagos Islands (Galapago being Spanish for tortoise)."

Again, "the air of these islands is temperate enough, considering the clime. Here is constantly a fresh sea-breeze all day, and cooling refreshing winds in the night; therefore the heat is not so violent here as in places near the equator."

"The time of the year for the rains is in November, December, and January: then there is oftentimes excessive dark tempestuous weather, mixed with much thunder and lightning. Sometimes before and after these months there are moderate refreshing showers; but in May, June, July, and August, the weather is always very fair."

"During the rainy season, or from November to March (which is not, however, at all to be compared to a continental rainy season) there are calms, variable breezes, and sometimes westerly winds: though the latter are neither of long duration, nor frequent."

I can add nothing to this excellent description, except that heavy rollers occasionally break upon the northern shores of the Galápagos during the rainy season above-mentioned—though no wind of any consequence accompanies them. They are caused by the 'Northers,' or 'Papagayos,' which are so well known on the coast between Panama and Acapulco.

Colnett also gives a good description of these islands:—in his *Voyage*, p. 58, he says, "I consider it as one of the most delightful climates under heaven, although situated within a few miles of the equator."

The buccaneers often resorted to them for refreshments, and as a place where they might refit their vessels, share out plunder, or plan new schemes of rapine, without any risk of being molested.

Striking instances of the manner in which high land deprives the air of its moisture may be seen at the Galápagos. Situated in a wind nearly perennial, those sides only which are exposed to it (the southern) are covered with verdure, and have water: all else is dry and barren, excepting such high ground as the passing clouds hang upon indolently as they move northward.

Charles Darwin and the Galapagos Islands

Charles Darwin, the young British naturalist who accompanied Captain FitzRoy on his historic survey voyage on HMS Beagle, *wrote and published much material about the Galapagos Islands over his lifetime. Although the animal and plant inhabitants of the Enchanted Isles interested him more, he did offer some observations about the archipelago's structure and climate. It's volcanic craters seemed to interest him greatly.*

A selection from Charles Darwin's Diary *of the voyage of HMS* Beagle, *25 September 1835* . . .

The main evil under which these islands suffer is the scarcity of water. — In very few places streams reach the beach so as to afford facilities for the watering of Shipping. Every where the porous nature of the Volcanic rocks has a tendency to absorb without again throwing up the little water which falls in the course of the year.

A selection from Charles Darwin's The Voyage of the Beagle, *Chapter XVII* . . .

September 15th.—This archipelago consists of ten principal islands, of which five exceed the others in size. They are situated under the Equator, and between five and six hundred miles westward of the coast of America. They are all formed of volcanic rocks; a few fragments of granite curiously glazed and altered by the heat can hardly be considered as an exception.

Some of the craters surmounting the larger islands are of immense size, and they rise to a height of between three and four thousand feet. Their flanks are studded by innumerable smaller orifices.

I scarcely hesitate to affirm that there must be in the whole archipelago at least two thousand craters. These consist either of lava and scoriae, or of finely-stratified, sandstone-like tuff. Most of the latter are beautifully symmetrical; they owe their origin to eruptions of volcanic mud without any lava: it is a remarkable circumstance that every one of the twenty-eight tuff-craters which were examined had their southern sides either much lower than the other sides, or quite broken down and removed.

As all these craters apparently have been formed when standing in the sea, and as the waves from the trade wind and the swells from the open Pacific here unite their forces on the southern coasts of all the islands, this singular uniformity in the broken state of the craters, composed of the soft and yielding tuff, is easily explained.

Considering that these islands are placed directly under the equator, the climate is far from being excessively hot; this seems chiefly caused by the singularly low temperature of the surrounding water, brought here by the great southern Polar current.

Excepting during one short season very little rain falls, and even then it is irregular; but the clouds generally hang low. Hence, whilst the lower parts of the islands are very sterile, the upper parts, at a height of a thousand feet and upwards, possess a damp climate and a tolerably luxuriant vegetation. This is especially the case on the windward sides of the islands, which first receive and condense the moisture from the atmosphere.

Herman Melville and the Galapagos Islands

Herman Melville's career started with such promise. His first two novels, Typee *(1846) and* Omoo *(1847), quickly became bestsellers.*

But Melville wanted to make a positive impact on the world with his writing. He began to focus on serious issues: political injustice, human cruelty, religious intolerance, slavery, racial bigotry, and the rigid sexual mores of his time.

The reading public loved exotic tales set in exotic locations. Strong heroic characters, direct action, romanticized locales, and suggestive "physicality" were popular literary motifs. Allegorical attacks on religious or political evils and innovative explorations of ambiguous aspects of the human condition most certainly were not.

Still determined to address important themes, Melville went on to write Moby-Dick *(1851) and* Pierre *(1852), losing readers with each new novel. "So much trash" and a "monstrous bore" proclaimed the nicest critics of* Moby-Dick. *Sales were poor.*

By January of 1854, Melville had begun to construct a series of ten magazine sketches—really an extended travelogue—full of myth and exotic scenery but still reflecting complex themes of good and evil that dominated his thoughts.

Once more he transported himself away from the snowy blasts that rattled his Massachusetts farmhouse; back twelve years and three thousand miles to the tropical South Seas of his youth. He published these as The Encantadas or Enchanted Isles.

Herman Melville clearly has no place writing travel brochures. His bleak depiction of volcanic Galapagos landscapes would certainly not entice tourists seeking a tropical paradise.

And he quickly dispels any Disney-like associations with the archipelago's nickname by conveying the understanding that Encantada *was used in its negative sense of "bewitched" rather than with any more joyful connotation.*

Yet this first of ten sketches describing the other-worldly environment of the Galapagos Islands (and beginning, like most of the ten, with a quote from Edmund Spenser's The Faerie Queen*), with its images of stark volcanic islands populated by demonic creatures—all probably a reflection of his own dark psyche—prepares visitors in an (almost) realistic way for their upcoming experiences.*

A selection from Melville's The Encantadas or Enchanted Isles . . .

SKETCH FIRST.
THE ISLES AT LARGE.

*—"That may not be, said then the ferryman,
Least we unweeting hap to be fordonne;
For those same islands seeming now and than,
Are not firme land, nor any certein wonne,
But stragling plots which to and fro do ronne
In the wide waters; therefore are they hight
The Wandering Islands; therefore do them shonne;
For they have oft drawne many a wandring wight
Into most deadly daunger and distressed plight;
For whosoever once hath fastened
His foot thereon may never it secure
But wandreth evermore uncertein and unsure."
"Darke, dolefull, dreary, like a greedy grave,
That still for carrion carcasses doth crave;
On top whereof ay dwelt the ghastly owl,
Shrieking his balefull note, which ever drave
Far from that haunt all other cheerful fowl,
And all about it wandring ghosts did wayle and howl."*

Take five-and-twenty heaps of cinders dumped here and there in an outside city lot; imagine some of them magnified into mountains, and the vacant lot the sea; and you will have a fit idea of the general aspect of the Encantadas, or Enchanted Isles. A group rather of extinct volcanoes than of isles; looking much as the world at large might, after a penal conflagration.

It is to be doubted whether any spot of earth can, in desolateness, furnish a parallel to this group. Abandoned cemeteries of long ago, old cities by piecemeal tumbling to their ruin, these are melancholy enough; but, like all else which has but once been associated with humanity, they still awaken in us some thoughts of sympathy, however sad. Hence, even the Dead Sea, along with whatever other emotions it may at times inspire, does not fail to touch in the pilgrim some of his less unpleasurable feelings.

And as for solitariness; the great forests of the north, the expanses of unnavigated waters, the Greenland ice-fields, are the profoundest of solitudes to a human observer; still the magic of their changeable tides and seasons mitigates their terror; because, though unvisited by men, those forests are visited by the May; the remotest seas reflect familiar stars even as Lake Erie does; and in the clear air of a fine Polar day, the irradiated, azure ice shows beautifully as malachite.

But the special curse, as one may call it, of the Encantadas, that which exalts them in desolation above Idumea and the Pole, is, that to them change never comes; neither the change of seasons nor of sorrows. Cut by the Equator, they know not autumn, and they know not spring; while already reduced to the lees of fire, ruin itself can work little more upon them.

The showers refresh the deserts; but in these isles, rain never falls. Like split Syrian gourds left withering in the sun, they are cracked by an everlasting drought beneath a torrid sky. "Have mercy upon me," the wailing spirit of the Encantadas seems to cry, "and send Lazarus that he may dip the tip of his finger in water and cool my tongue, for I am tormented in this flame."

Another feature in these isles is their emphatic uninhabitableness. It is deemed a fit type of all-forsaken overthrow, that the jackal should den in the wastes of weedy Babylon; but the Encantadas refuse to harbor even the outcasts of the beasts. Man and wolf alike disown them.

Little but reptile life is here found: tortoises, lizards, immense spiders, snakes, and that strangest anomaly of outlandish nature, the *aguano*. No voice, no low, no howl is heard; the chief sound of life here is a hiss.

On most of the isles where vegetation is found at all, it is more ungrateful than the blankness of *Aracama*. Tangled thickets of wiry bushes, without fruit and without a name, springing up among deep fissures of calcined rock, and treacherously masking them; or a parched growth of distorted cactus trees.

In many places the coast is rock-bound, or, more properly, clinker-bound; tumbled masses of blackish or greenish stuff like the dross of an iron-furnace, forming dark clefts and caves here and there, into which a ceaseless sea pours a fury of foam; overhanging them with a swirl of gray, haggard mist, amidst which sail screaming flights of unearthly birds heightening the dismal din. However calm the sea without, there is no rest for these swells and those rocks; they lash and are lashed, even when the outer ocean is most at peace with, itself.

On the oppressive, clouded days, such as are peculiar to this part of the watery Equator, the dark, vitrified masses, many of which raise themselves among white whirlpools and breakers in detached and perilous places off the shore, present a most Plutonian sight. In no world but a fallen one could such lands exist.

Those parts of the strand free from the marks of fire, stretch away in wide level beaches of multitudinous dead shells, with here and there decayed bits of sugar-cane, bamboos, and cocoanuts, washed upon this other and darker world from the charming palm isles to the westward and southward; all the way from Paradise to Tartarus; while mixed with the relics of distant beauty you will sometimes see fragments of charred wood and mouldering ribs of wrecks.

Neither will any one be surprised at meeting these last, after observing the conflicting currents which eddy throughout nearly all the wide channels of the entire group. The capriciousness of the tides of air sympathizes with those of the sea. Nowhere is the wind so light, baffling, and every way unreliable, and so given to perplexing calms, as at the Encantadas.

Nigh a month has been spent by a ship going from one isle to another, though but ninety miles between; for owing to the force of the current, the boats employed to tow barely suffice to keep the craft from sweeping upon the cliffs, but do nothing towards accelerating her voyage.

Sometimes it is impossible for a vessel from afar to fetch up with the group itself, unless large allowances for prospective lee-way have been made ere its coming in sight. And yet, at other times, there is a mysterious indraft, which irresistibly draws a passing vessel among the isles, though not bound to them.

True, at one period, as to some extent at the present day, large fleets of whalemen cruised for spermaceti upon what some seamen call the Enchanted Ground. But this, as in due place will be described, was off the great outer isle of Albemarle [Isabela], away from the intricacies of the smaller isles, where there is plenty of sea-room; and hence, to that vicinity, the above remarks do not altogether apply; though even there the current runs at times with singular force, shifting, too, with as singular a caprice.

Indeed, there are seasons when currents quite unaccountable prevail for a great distance round about the total group, and are so strong and irregular as to change a vessel's course against the helm, though sailing at the rate of four or five miles the hour.

The difference in the reckonings of navigators, produced by these causes, along with the light and variable winds, long nourished a persuasion, that there existed two distinct clusters of isles in the parallel of the Encantadas, about a hundred leagues apart. Such was the idea of their earlier visitors, the Buccaneers; and as late as 1750, the charts of that part of the Pacific accorded with the strange delusion. And this apparent fleetingness and unreality of the locality of the isles was most probably one reason for the Spaniards calling them the Encantada, or Enchanted Group.

But not uninfluenced by their character, as they now confessedly exist, the modern voyager will be inclined to fancy that the bestowal of this name might have in part originated in that air of spell-bound desertness which so significantly invests the isles. Nothing can better suggest the aspect of once living things malignly crumbled from ruddiness into ashes. Apples of Sodom, after touching, seem these isles.

However wavering their place may seem by reason of the currents, they themselves, at least to one upon the shore, appear invariably the same: fixed, cast, glued into the very body of cadaverous death.

Nor would the appellation, enchanted, seem misapplied in still another sense. For concerning the peculiar reptile inhabitant of these wilds—whose presence gives the group its second Spanish name, Gallipagos—concerning the tortoises found here, most mariners have long cherished a superstition, not more frightful than grotesque. They earnestly believe that all wicked sea-officers, more especially commodores and captains, are at death (and, in some cases, before death) transformed into tortoises; thenceforth dwelling upon these hot aridities, sole solitary lords of Asphaltum.

Doubtless, so quaintly dolorous a thought was originally inspired by the woe-begone landscape itself; but more particularly, perhaps, by the tortoises. For, apart from their strictly physical features, there is something strangely self-condemned in the appearance of these creatures. Lasting sorrow and penal hopelessness are in no animal form so suppliantly expressed as in theirs; while the thought of their wonderful longevity does not fail to enhance the impression.

Nor even at the risk of meriting the charge of absurdly believing in enchantments, can I restrain the admission that sometimes, even now, when leaving the crowded city to wander out July and August among the Adirondack Mountains, far from the influences of towns and proportionally nigh to the mysterious ones of nature; when at such times I sit me down in the mossy head of some deep-wooded gorge, surrounded by prostrate trunks of blasted pines and recall, as in a dream, my other and far-distant rovings in the baked heart of the charmed isles; and remember the sudden glimpses of dusky shells, and long languid necks protruded from the leafless thickets; and again have beheld the vitreous inland rocks worn down and grooved into deep ruts by ages and ages of the slow draggings of tortoises in quest of pools of scanty water; I can hardly resist the feeling that in my time I have indeed slept upon evilly enchanted ground.

Nay, such is the vividness of my memory, or the magic of my fancy, that I know not whether I am not the occasional victim of optical delusion concerning the Gallipagos.

For, often in scenes of social merriment, and especially at revels held by candle-light in old-fashioned mansions, so that shadows are thrown into the further recesses of an angular and spacious room, making them put on a look of haunted undergrowth of lonely woods, I have drawn the attention of my comrades by my fixed gaze and sudden change of air, as I have seemed to see, slowly emerging from those imagined solitudes, and heavily crawling along the floor, the ghost of a gigantic tortoise, with "Memento * * * * *" burning in live letters upon his back.

Photo Gallery: Landscapes

These photographs by Moses Michelsohn reflect the diversity of geology and plant life found throughout the Galapagos Archipelago.

Sunlight strikes weathered remnants of volcanic craters.

Bright orange Sally Lightfoot Crabs forage around a tide pool along a rough black lava shoreline.

Opuntia trees grow along a rocky shore.

Guano-streaked cliffs rise from the depths.

Two sea lions emerge from the sea onto the white sandy beach of a protected cove.

Greenery struggles to survive inside a collapsed lava tube.

A bromeliad overlooks the floor of a vast volcanic crater on Isla Isabela, the island early visitors knew as Albemarle.

Vegetation flourishes at higher elevations.

Plants struggle to survive, even on this harsh volcanic slope.

Mangroves with their twisted roots grow in salt water shallows along a lava shoreline.

Biologists Peter and Rosemary Grant studied Darwin's finches on Daphne Major (on the left) for more than 20 years, as described in the book, *The Beak of the Finch*. Daphne Minor is on the right.

Bird droppings spot a field of boulders.

Frozen layers of lava cover a lowland.

A Note on Island Names

Each of the Galapagos Islands has several names, a heritage of their centuries of human history.

Names assigned by English buccaneers in the 1600s generally superseded those used by early Spanish explorers, except for the name of the archipelago itself, "The Galapagos Islands" (referring to the saddle shape of the tortoise shells). Fray Tomas de Berlanga, Bishop of Panama, first referred the islands in this fashion in 1535. (Actually the official name is Archipelago de Colon but no one uses this.)

Captain William Ambrosia Cowley, an English buccaneer, explorer, adventurer, and writer who visited the Galápagos Islands while sailing around the world in the mid-1600s, named individual islands after British royalty and aristocrats. As he published the first widely used chart of the archipelago in 1684, these names quickly came into common usage.

When Ecuador annexed the archipelago in 1832 the new government assigned each island an official Spanish name, often that of a Catholic saint. These are the names commonly used today, although a few islands picked up other common names along the way.

Melville briefly mentions the islands of Abington (Pinta), Brattle (Tortuga), Chatham (San Cristobal), Cowley's Enchanted (Cowley), Crossman's (several possible islets), Duncan (Pinzon), Jervis (Rabida) and Wood's (also Santa Maria).

The primary islands described in *The Encantadas* are:

Older Name	Today's Name
Albemarle	Isabela
Barrington	Santa Fe
Charles's	Santa Maria, Floreana
Hood's	Española
James's	San Salvador, Santiago
Narborough	Fernandina
Norfolk	Santa Cruz

**Have you have enjoyed these glimpses
of the Galapagos Islands?**

If so, please help others find our book.

~ Do you have friends who are interested in the Galapagos Islands? Tell them about this book, or purchase copies for them—ebooks or paperbacks.

~ Mention *Galapagos Landscapes* in your Tweets, or on your Facebook page, blog, or other social media.

~ Write a review—no matter how brief—of *Galapagos Landscapes* on the website where you purchased this book. Add your review to other reader or bookseller websites.

~ Comments or questions?
Contact the author at:
2LynnMichelsohn@gmail.com

See Lynn Michelsohn's other books about the Galapagos Islands:
Galapagos Birds, *In the Galapagos Islands with Herman Melville*, and
The Chola Widow

For more information about the Galapagos Islands
and our other books, visit our website:

www.cleananpressBooks.com

**Thank you,
For reading our book,
and
for your help
in letting others know about it!**

Acknowledgements

"The Geography of Herman Melville" in John Woram's enjoyable book *Charles Darwin Slept Here* provided a variety of interesting information as did *Critical Companion to Herman Melville* by Carl Rollyson, Lisa Paddock, and April Gentry. Hershel Parker's two volume *Herman Melville: A Biography* furnished detailed information about Melville's time in the Galapagos Islands, as well as the months he spent writing "The Encantadas."

All quotes from contemporary reviews of Melville's novels came from the highly detailed and immensely readable *Melville, A Biography* by Laurie Robertson-Lorant.

We thank Dr. David Hastings for leading a great trip to the Galapagos Islands, Aaron Michelsohn for his valuable editorial assistance, and Larry Michelsohn for his continued support of this and all our projects.

About the Illustrations

The period drawings included in this work come from an illustrated 1890 edition of Charles Darwin's *The Voyage of the Beagle*, a narrative first published in 1839, about the time Herman Melville was sailing the South Pacific.

Moses Michelsohn took all the photographs for this book in the Galapagos Islands.

About the Authors

In 1859, **Charles Darwin** (1809-1882) published his theory of Evolution by Natural Selection inspired especially by the diversity of plants and animals he saw on the various Galapagos Islands during his time as naturalist on HMS *Beagle*.

Royal Navy career officer **Captain Robert FitzRoy** (1805-1865), commander of HMS Beagle during its 1831-1836 round-the-world survey mission, remained a committed Creationist throughout his life, strongly opposed to Darwin's Theory of Evolution.

Herman Melville (1819-1891) wrote this selection from "The Encantadas," like *Moby-Dick* and "Billy Budd," by drawing on his shipboard experiences in the South Seas as a young sailor.

Author **Lynn Michelsohn** enjoys tracking down details of interesting places and characters, both well represented in the Galapagos Islands. Although they like traveling, she and her husband split most of their time between Santa Fe, New Mexico, and Hutchinson Island, Florida.

Biologist and nature photographer **Moses Michelsohn** found the Galapagos Islands fascinating, but tree frogs in Ecuador, Costa Rica, and the southeastern United States remain his primary research interest.

Other Books by Lynn Michelsohn

Most are available as both paperback and ebook

In the Galapagos Islands . . .

Galapagos Birds
Wildlife Photographs of Moses Michelsohn,
words of Melville, Darwin, and FitzRoy
(Galapagos Islands Nature Series)

The Chola Widow
Herman Melville's Short Story of
Death and Rape in the Galapagos Islands

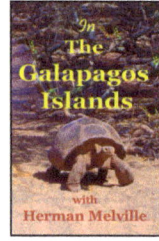

In the Galapagos Islands with Herman Melville
Tour the Galapagos Islands with the author of *Moby-Dick*,
Nature photography by Moses Michelsohn

In the American Southwest . . .

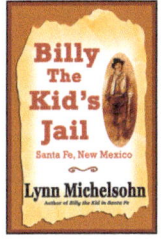  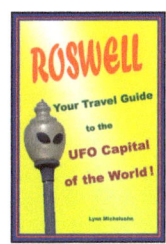 

Folklore, Ghost Stories, Gullah Folktales of the Carolina Lowcountry . . .

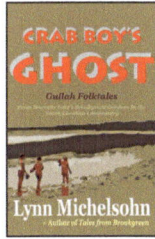   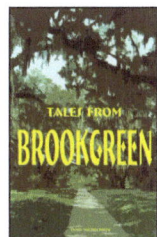

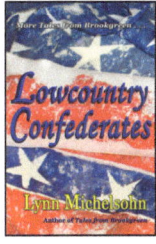